12/16

A Beginning-to-Read Book

In the Sky

by Mary Lindeen

NORWOOD HOUSE PRESS

DEAR CAREGIVER, The *Beginning to Read—Read and Discover* books provide emergent readers the opportunity to explore the world through nonfiction while building early reading skills. The text integrates both common sight words and content vocabulary. These key words are featured on lists provided at the back of the book to help your child expand his or her sight word recognition, which helps build reading fluency. The content words expand vocabulary and support comprehension.

Nonfiction text is any text that is factual. The Common Core State Standards call for an increase in the amount of informational text reading among students. The Standards aim to promote college and career readiness among students. Preparation for college and career endeavors requires proficiency in reading complex informational texts in a variety of content areas. You can help your child build a foundation by introducing nonfiction early. To further support the CCSS, you will find Reading Reinforcement activities at the back of the book that are aligned to these Standards.

Above all, the most important part of the reading experience is to have fun and enjoy it!

Sincerely,

Shannon Cannon

Shannon Cannon, Ph.D.
Literacy Consultant

Norwood House Press • P.O. Box 316598 • Chicago, Illinois 60631
For more information about Norwood House Press please visit our website at
www.norwoodhousepress.com or call 866-565-2900.
© 2016 Norwood House Press. Beginning-to-Read™ is a trademark of Norwood House Press.
All rights reserved. No part of this book may be reproduced or utilized in any form or by any
means without written permission from the publisher.

Editor: Judy Kentor Schmauss
Designer: Lindaanne Donohoe

Photo Credits:

Shutterstock, cover, 1, 3, 4-5, 6, 7, 8-9 (nitinut380), 10-11, 14-15, 18-19, 20-21, 22, 23, 24-25, 28-29; Phil Martin, 12-13, 16-17, 26-27

Library of Congress Cataloging-in-Publication Data
    Lindeen, Mary.
    In the sky / by Mary Lindeen.
        pages cm. – (A beginning to read book)
    Audience: K to Grade 3.
    Summary: "Look up in the sky. You can see birds, airplanes, clouds, and lights.
You can see the sun and the moon. Sometimes you can even see fireworks! This
title includes reading activities and a word list"– Provided by publisher.
    ISBN 978-1-59953-696-5 (library edition : alk. paper)
    ISBN 978-1-60357-781-6 (ebook)
    1. Sky–Juvenile literature. I. Title.
    QC863.5.L57 2015
    551.5–dc23
                              2015001227

Manufactured in the United States of America in Stevens Point, Wisconsin. 275N-062015

Look up!

What do you see in the sky?

The sun is in the sky.

It keeps us warm.

It gives us light.

Birds are in the sky, too.

They use their wings to fly.

Airplanes are in the sky.

They have wings, too.

Sometimes clouds are in the sky.

These clouds are white and puffy.

These clouds are dark.

They are full of rain.

Time to go in the house!

The rain is over.

Now there is a
rainbow in the sky.

The moon is in the sky at night.

Sometimes it looks big and round like this.

This bird is flying
in the night sky.

It is an owl.

Airplanes can fly at night, too.

They use lights.

Look at all of these lights.

They are fireflies.

Fireflies have their own lights.

Do you know what
these lights are?

They are up very
high in the sky.

They are stars.

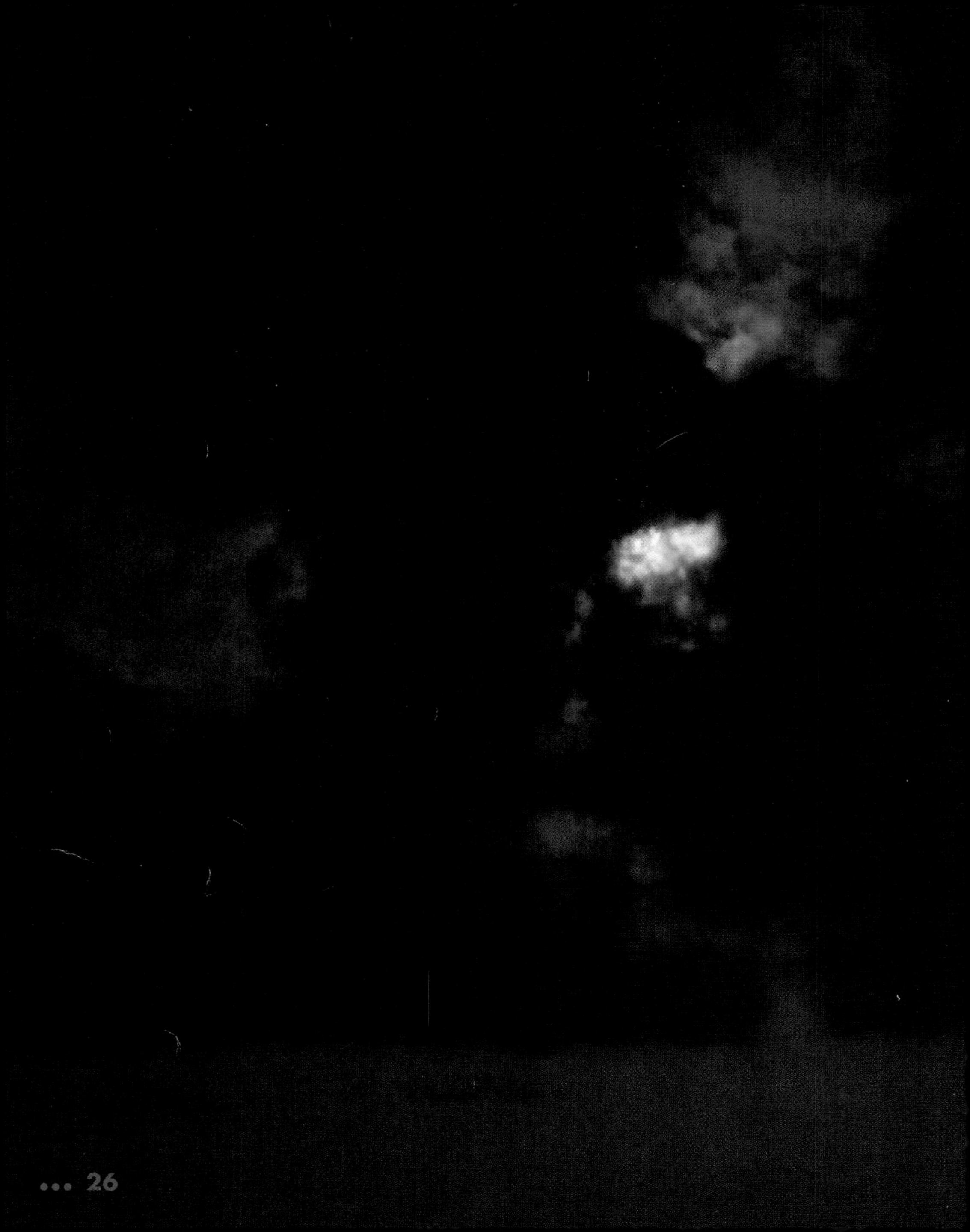

Sometimes there are clouds in the night sky.

Then you can not see the stars.

There are no clouds now.

There is something else in the sky!

What do you see?

...READING REINFORCEMENT...

CRAFT AND STRUCTURE

To check your child's understanding of this book, recreate the following diagram on a sheet of paper. Read the book with your child, then help him or her fill in the diagram using what they learned. Work together to complete the diagram by writing the main idea of this book and several details relating to it:

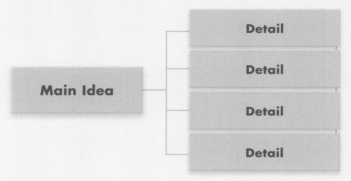

VOCABULARY: Learning Content Words

Content words are words that are specific to a particular topic. All of the content words for this book can be found on page 32. Use some or all of these content words to complete one or more of the following activities:

- Write each compound word (two words joined to make another word) from the Content Word List (see page 32) on a note card. Cut each compound word card apart to make the two smaller words, mix up the cards, and have your child put them back together to make the compound words.

- Provide clues about the meaning of a content word, and have your child guess the word.

- Write the content words on slips of paper. Place them in a box. Have your child pick a word and use it in a sentence.

- Help your child use content words to make up similes (using the word like or as to make a comparison); for example, It was like night in the tunnel or The tunnel was as dark as night.

- Act out a content word and have your child guess the word. Switch roles.

FOUNDATIONAL SKILLS: Compound words

A compound word is formed when two or more words are put together to make a new word. The new word has a new meaning. Have your child identify the compound words in the list below. Then ask your child to find compound words in this book.

puffy	rainbow	owl
airplanes	hoot	fireflies
clouds	rain	sometimes

CLOSE READING OF INFORMATIONAL TEXT

Close reading helps children comprehend text. It includes reading a text, discussing it with others, and answering questions about it. Use these questions to discuss this book with your child:

- What are three things you can see in the sky?
- How are airplanes and birds alike? Different?
- What might happen if dark clouds are in the sky?
- What is the difference between rain and a rainbow?
- What would happen if you could fly through the sky?
- Would it be better if people had their own lights like fireflies? Why or why not?

FLUENCY

Fluency is the ability to read accurately with speed and expression. Help your child practice fluency by using one or more of the following activities:

- Reread this book to your child at least two times while he or she uses a finger to track each word as you read it.
- Read the first sentence aloud. Then have your child reread the sentence with you. Continue until you have finished this book.
- Ask your child to read aloud the words they know on each page of this book. (Your child will learn additional words with subsequent readings.)
- Have your child practice reading this book several times to improve accuracy, rate, and expression.

••• Word List •••

In the Sky uses the 68 words listed below. *High-frequency* words are those words that are used most often in the English language. They are sometimes referred to as sight words because children need to learn to recognize them automatically when they read. *Content words* are any words specific to a particular topic. Regular practice reading these words will enhance your child's ability to read with greater fluency and comprehension.

High-Frequency Words

a	gives	like	something	to
all	go	look(s)	the	too
an	have	no	their	up
and	high	not	then	us
are	house	now	there	use
at	in	of	these	very
big	is	over	they	what
can	it	own	this	you
do	know	see	time	

Content Words

airplanes	fireflies	moon	rainbow	sun
bird(s)	fly(ing)	night	round	warm
clouds	full	owl	sky	white
dark	keeps	puffy	sometimes	wings
else	light(s)	rain	stars	

••• About the Author

Mary Lindeen is a writer, editor, parent, and former elementary school teacher. She has written more than 100 books for children and edited many more. She specializes in early literacy instruction and books for young readers, especially nonfiction.

••• About the Advisor

Dr. Shannon Cannon is a teacher educator in the School of Education at UC Davis, where she also earned her Ph.D. in Language, Literacy, and Culture. She serves on the clinical faculty, supervising pre-service teachers and teaching elementary methods courses in reading, effective teaching, and teacher action research.